simple Solutions
Living Spaces

simpleSolutions
Living Spaces

JESSICA TOLLIVER

Foreword by Timothy Drew
Managing Editor, *Home Magazine*

FRIEDMAN/FAIRFAX

A FRIEDMAN/FAIRFAX BOOK
© 2002 by Michael Friedman Publishing Group, Inc.

Please visit our website: www.metrobooks.com

Library of Congress Cataloging-in-Publication Data

Tolliver, Jessica.
    Living spaces / by Jessica Tolliver.
       p. ; cm. – (Simple solutions)
    Includes bibliographical references and index.
    ISBN 1-58663-570-0 (alk. paper)
     1. Living rooms. 2. Recreation rooms. 3. Interior decoration. I. Title. II.
    SimpleSolutions.

    NK2117.L5 T65 2002 2002
    747'.88—dc21

2002020687

Editor: Hallie Einhorn
Art Director: Midori Nakamura
Designer: Orit Mardkha-Tenzer
Photography Editor: Lori Epstein
Production Manager: Michael Vagnetti

Color separations by Bright Arts Graphics (Singapore) Pte Ltd.
Printed in China by C&C Offset Printing Co., Ltd.

10 9 8 7 6 5 4 3 2 1

Distributed by Sterling Publishing Company, Inc.
387 Park Avenue South
New York, NY 10016
Distributed in Canada by Sterling Publishing
Canadian Manda Group
One Atlantic Avenue, Suite 105
Toronto, Ontario, Canada M6K 3E7
Distributed in Australia by
Capricorn Link (Australia) Pty, Ltd.
P.O. Box 704, Windsor, NSW 2756 Australia

Acknowledgments

To Josie's grandmothers, who provided hours of babysitting services: Thank you!
And thanks to Tim Drew.

Contents

Foreword

Assemble a panel of ten people, let's say five women and five men, of varying generations. Now, ask each of them for a description of what the ideal living space should be. Lo and behold, the complexity of human needs, wants, and tastes is made evident. But truth be told, this wide array of opinions probably only scratches the surface of our differing expectations.

Maybe it would help if we define what we think a living space is. For many, the traditional term "living room" brings to mind a latter-day version of the old-fashioned parlor, which was hardly a space where anyone "lived." Rather, it was a formal room reserved for special occasions. Today, however, the term "living room," like the more contemporary phrase "living space," has come to describe the place where we hang out after the dishes are done, where we relax, where we gather with friends, or simply where we like to be.

And what are we doing when we're enjoying our living spaces? Well, it seems almost anything: watching television or a movie, listening to music, chatting, meditating, playing games, entertaining guests, or maybe just watching the snow fall. This is quite a gamut of activities, some of which would seem to be mutually exclusive.

In our space-planning considerations, deciding what we want often depends on knowing what we don't want. Experience can have a lot to say on the matter. As an early precursor of the boomerang generation (the contemporary term for offspring who, once finished with college, return home to deprive their parents of the quiet pleasures of an empty nest), I could happily be ensconced in my parents' den, listening to a record—yes, a record—playing softly on the Magnavox console stereo, when my father would stroll in, flip on the tube, and believe it or not, manually turn the channels looking for any John Wayne movie. Since the stereo was about three feet (91cm) from the television, it struck me that maybe we expected far too much from one little den.

Well, the point is that planning is key. Careful consideration must be given to how we, both as individuals and as families, intend to use our living spaces. Today's multipurpose open floor plans are ideal for many of our needs, but sometimes certain activities call for special spaces. A case in point could be whether a separate room for the home-theater equipment is necessary. Personally, I'd vote yes, but I will concede that a family of cinephiles dedicated to the oeuvre of John Wayne could be deliriously happy with a combined dining room and home theater.

Ideally, getting it right shouldn't be a matter of making a lot of mistakes first. Such a process could be a tad frustrating, not to mention costly. Instead, look around at what others have done. What do you like—and not like—about the results? Keep a file of ideas. Fortunately, you have in your hands a valuable resource. In *Simple Solutions: Living Spaces,* author Jessica Tolliver has done much of your homework for you. Of course, visually there's plenty to inspire your own creativity, but just as importantly, the author both explains why a space is successful and points out the details that make it work so well.

Here's hoping your living spaces are every bit as livable as you want them to be.

Timothy Drew
Managing Editor, *Home Magazine*

Introduction

Some call it the living room, some the family room. Still others settle for monikers like "great room," "parlor," or "sitting room." The parade of names used to describe the living areas in our homes goes on. Fitting perhaps, because the list of functions performed by these spaces is equally lengthy. In most residences, the living room—or whatever you choose to call it—must play at least some of the following roles: receiving area, gathering space, cinema and music hall, playroom, game room, home office, library.

The needs and lifestyles of the homeowners, of course, determine which of these services their living areas will provide. In one home, for example, residents may want a cozy parlorlike space, outfitted with oversize chairs and proper lighting for reading—a room conducive to quiet relaxation. In a home with small children, though, a living area with storage for toys, child-friendly surfaces, and ample room for play may be desired. Some people require a space that is suitable for entertaining business colleagues, others for hosting gatherings with friends and family on a fairly regular basis. And, of course, most people today spend a significant amount of time watching television and want a comfortable spot in which to do so.

When designing a living space, you must above all take into account your own needs. Before you contemplate traditional versus contemporary or chintz versus chinoiserie, you should consider your living habits. What pleases you most? What brings your family comfort and emotional nourishment? Design a room that responds to the answers to these questions, and it, no doubt, will be a success.

While today's living areas are shaped by the individual requirements and tastes of their owners, these spaces still possess a number of common qualities. Many of the shared traits stem from similarities in lifestyle. In fact, as lifestyles evolved over the years, so too did the faces of our living areas.

During the past few decades, for example, Americans gradually shifted from a formal way of life to a more casual one—and the living spaces in our homes reflect this change. During the 1950s, a few forward-thinking architects and designers noticed a sea change in how people were occupying their homes; children were coming out of their bedrooms and joining family members downstairs, and guests were being welcomed into the more informal rooms, such as the kitchen.

In an effort to build houses that would accommodate these new tendencies, architects designed casual living areas that opened onto the dining area and sometimes the kitchen. No longer removed from the other activity centers of the home, these revolutionary living spaces promoted togetherness, bringing together many pursuits—including cooking, eating, and socializing—within the boundaries of a single large room.

Several decades later, this formerly novel concept has become the status quo. Not only do most new residences feature casual, open-plan living areas, but many old homes are being remodeled to include such spaces as well. Today, family members want to spend their time at home in close proximity to one another, and they expect the layout of their dwellings to facilitate this goal. So, the oft-painted picture of modern family life—members sharing a single space, even if the children are watching television and the parents are cooking dinner—is certainly a reality.

As the fledgling twenty-first century progresses, the design of our living areas continues to evolve. Televisions are growing larger, and entertainment systems are becoming more complex. As a result, many homeowners are searching for solutions to the problem of seamlessly integrating these cumbersome—yet cherished—components into their spaces. Similarly, the computer is assuming an ever-expanding role in home life. As people spend more time online, they no longer want the computer to be tucked away in a remote bedroom. Like the television, they want to incorporate it into their living spaces so that individuals can feel a part of the family whole, even when checking e-mail.

No matter how our living areas change in the years to come, their basic role will most likely remain the same. We retreat to these spaces at the end of our workdays and school days to relax and regroup. Here, we visit, we entertain, we complete homework and craft projects, we watch television, and we read. In sum, we look to these rooms as the backdrop for the cornucopia of leisure activities that compose our daily lives.

Many books and magazines on design often resort to the phrase "heart of the home" to describe the kitchen. Not to belittle the role of the kitchen, but our living areas shoulder a responsibility that is equally significant. They are, after all, the rooms we turn to when all the chores are complete, when we have the freedom to take off our shoes and prop up our feet. If the title "heart of the home" is already taken, the living room deserves another. "Soul of the home" certainly sounds appropriate.

Jessica Tolliver

Open-Plan Living

or most families, gone are the times of Mom cooking dinner in the kitchen, Dad reading the paper in the study, and the children playing games in their bedrooms. After busy days at school and work, we want to spend our hours at home **together**, not apart. Open-plan spaces offer the best of both worlds, allowing family members to do their own thing while enjoying one another's company. But whether the space is a living-dining area or a great room (the latter combining a living area, dining area, and kitchen), these types of floor plans present **challenges**. If not carefully designed, the vast expanses can seem overwhelming instead of welcoming. And while different activity zones benefit from a sense of definition, they must **coexist** harmoniously.

bright ideas

▶ Select different flooring materials for different zones

▶ Lower the ceiling over the kitchen for a sense of intimacy

▶ Install cabinets on the living room side of an island for storage of games and books

In this home, the living and dining areas share a large common space. A set of open shelves stands between the two zones to create a sense of division without obstructing sight lines. ➲

Partial walls set off the adjacent kitchen without completely enclosing it. Columns of glass block maintain the wide-open feeling of the space.

A slightly translucent screen shields the view of the kitchen from this living area while still permitting the passage of light and maintaining a sense of openness. Mounted on casters, the screen can be moved to the side to allow for more ready visiting between the two activity centers. ⌒

Thanks to a skillful use of color and form, the furnishings in this open-plan space coexist harmoniously yet give each area a feeling of individuality. Curving lines visually link the living area's seating with the dining chairs and the bar stools; similarly, the presence of the same type of wood in the kitchen island, dining table, and coffee table helps to tie the different activity zones together. However, slight shifts in the color scheme—the addition of bold hues in the living area, the use of all neutrals in the dining area, and the appearance of black in the kitchen—give each space a distinct flair. ☊

A change in flooring further defines the living area. The wood planks beneath the seating arrangement stand out not only because they have been stained a much darker shade than the bulk of the floorboards, but also because they have been laid in a different direction. The round shape of the flooring inset complements the curves that repeat throughout the room. ◑

Thanks to a clever design strategy, this open-plan space functions as three different rooms. A large round table takes up residence between the dining room and living area, creating a border between the two. Much like the tables found in more conventional entryways, the classical piece also creates the impression of a foyer for those entering from the front or back of the house. ♩

Columns set off the front door from the rest of the space.

French doors and a row of windows break down the barriers between inside and out, bringing the natural landscape into the decor. Up toward the ceiling, a second configuration of windows recalls the fluidity of the sea beyond with its undulating shape. ↻

Using contrasting finishes for cabinetry—a dark stain in the living area and light-colored paint in the kitchen—helps to differentiate between activity zones.

Columns and a change in floor level define the boundaries of this living space without closing it off. The design results in a feeling of spaciousness and allows light to flow freely between the different areas. ◑

While the architectural proportions of this house give it a grand demeanor, the open layout fosters a relaxed mood. Comfortable furnishings enhance the laid-back tone. ↻

With its back to the dining area, the couch acts as a subtle divider. A sofa table reinforces the boundary.

In this great room, the kitchen is hidden behind a half wall of wooden panels. The thoughtful design feature allows occupants of the living area to converse with the chef—without being subjected to a view of messy pots and pans. ☊

The geometric configuration of the divider turns this functional asset into an exciting design feature.

The upbeat mood of the living area extends into the dining space, thanks to a similar use of color. With the distinct activity zones just steps away from one another, diners can effortlessly retire to the sitting area after a meal and continue the conversation with family members cleaning up in the kitchen. ◑

With its soaring windows and sliding glass doors, this vast great room seems even larger as it merges with the landscape beyond. Despite the massive proportions of the space, the sitting area manages a sense of intimacy. This feeling has been achieved by clustering the furnishings in front of a striking fireplace—an amenity that provides warmth both literally and figuratively. ☾

The wraparound design of the fireplace allows it to be enjoyed from both the sitting area and the dining area.

Details on both the floor and ceiling lend definition to the living and dining areas in this long stretch of a great room. The ceiling beams in the dining space run perpendicular to those in the sitting area, providing a subtle form of differentiation. Underfoot, area rugs help to anchor each zone. ◑

Fireplaces in the living room and the dining area give each space its own focal point. The feeling of coziness provided by these amenities is enhanced by the intimate furniture groupings. ◗

Casual Family Rooms

In many homes, particularly older ones, space constraints dictate that the everyday gathering area be separated from the home's other activity centers. But whether this family room is the one and only living space—used for both entertaining guests and daily relaxation—or a casual **retreat** that exists in addition to a more formal living room, it can be just as comfortable and **accommodating** as its open-plan counterparts. No longer bastions of polite conversation and coffee cups perched on knees, today's family rooms host raucous football parties, children's craft projects, and Saturday afternoon naps on the sofa.

bright ideas

▶ Call upon baskets to store reading materials

▶ Incorporate plenty of tables for drinks and snacks

▶ Add floor pillows for comfy lounging

A colorful palette, comfortable seating, and playful wall hangings give this room its casual, welcoming demeanor. On a practical note, the coffee table is sturdy and expansive enough to withstand spilled sodas and host rousing card games. ➲

A bookshelf provides storage for an overflow of kitchen items. Carefully edited to reflect the family room's color scheme, the contents of the shelves become decorative accents.

Awash in the fresh hues of blue and white, this airy family room takes its design inspiration from the easy languor of the seaside. The slipcover on the chair and the area rug underfoot can easily be thrown in the wash, thereby imbuing the room with a worry-free atmosphere. A cloth over the coffee table protects the surface from scratches. ☊

An L-shaped sofa wraps around one corner of this family room, encouraging conversation and fostering a sense of intimacy. Although the relatively large piece consumes a substantial amount of floor space, the high ceiling prevents the room from feeling cramped. ↻

A wall-mounted speaker blends into the background, filling the room with music without intruding upon the decor.

Tucked into a mezzanine overlooking the primary living space, this informal sitting area provides a cozy place to chat or read. Outfitted with cushy seating, oversize throw pillows, and an ottoman that doubles as a coffee table, the snug retreat promises rest and relaxation. ⋔

Careful planning transformed a tiny sliver of extra floor space into an inviting gathering area. Built-in seating—an oft-used space-saving solution for tight quarters—takes advantage of every nook and cranny along the edge of the area without crowding the room. ⍑

Windows—even those that overlook another part of the house—can prevent a small space from feeling confined.

The huge scale of the home's primary living space, located on the main floor, contrasts sharply with the intimacy of the upstairs sitting area. Impressive as they may be, grand surroundings can feel overwhelming at times. In such instances, a small, comfortable enclave can be a much-appreciated retreat. ◑

This highly accommodating family room was carved out of an attic. Complete with a pool table and an entertainment system, the space is geared toward hours of fun and relaxation. A splash of aqua on the ceiling and a sunny arched window make the room bright and cheery, while a fireplace provides comfort on winter nights. ⋒

Equipped with a sink, a mini-refrigerator, and a microwave, a kitchenette keeps plenty of refreshments close at hand, eliminating any need to retreat to the full-fledged kitchen. A small desk in the corner allows family members to surf the Internet and check e-mail— also without ever needing to leave the room. ➲

A built-in window bench offers a cozy perch for time alone and taking in the view.

Rooms for Entertaining

In a time of ever-lengthening workdays and jam-packed schedules, we are turning to our homes for comfort more than ever. We are welcoming family, friends, and colleagues into our homes for gatherings both formal and informal, when before we might have automatically headed out the door for a night on the town. Ideally, our living spaces will accommodate these get-togethers in comfort and style, providing ample space for mingling, furniture arrangements that encourage conversation, and surfaces for keeping a generous supply of refreshments on hand.

bright ideas

- Create multiple conversation areas
- Include several tables that can act as serving stations
- Select some furnishings that can be rearranged easily to accommodate guests

Located so close to the living area, this kitchen island is the perfect place to set out a buffet during parties. Plus, guests can line up inside the kitchen to get their meals, thereby avoiding congestion in the living area. ➲

When guests come over for dinner, they can congregate in this family room, which is located just beyond the island of the kitchen. The arrangement allows visitors to talk to the chef without interrupting preparations or getting underfoot. They can even pull a stool up to the counter to enjoy an appetizer or lend a hand. ⌒

During dinner parties and other gatherings, a trolley can be called into service as a temporary bar. Featuring casters, this type of furnishing can effortlessly be moved to where it is needed most. Handy and versatile, the trolley allows guests to help themselves, thereby simplifying the host's responsibilities. ☉

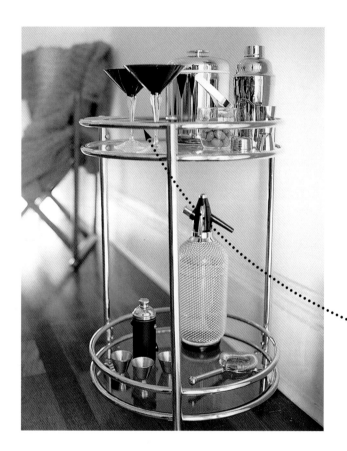

A raised edge acts as a guardrail to prevent objects from falling off when the trolley is moved.

The two-story wall of windows and soaring vaulted ceiling in this great room serve as an impressive backdrop during get-togethers, both large and small. The sprawling floor plan and sparse furnishings provide guests with plenty of room to mingle without feeling crowded. A counter between the dining area and the kitchen can function conveniently as a bar. ➲

Overlooking the main floor, the bedroom shares in the bounty of natural light flooding into the public areas of the home. A pair of doors can be pulled shut to provide privacy when company calls.

The plush furnishings in this room offer guests comfortable spots upon which to settle when socializing. Generously proportioned side tables include plenty of room for a drink and a dinner plate, while the ottoman can hold a tray of appetizers or a bowl of chips. ◑

The variety of seating options in this living room will make guests feel at home, no matter what their preference: stretching out on the chaise longue, exchanging confidences on the love seat, or engaging in a group discussion on the sofa. The small end tables can be moved around easily as needs dictate. ➲

Recessed in a small alcove, a wet bar stands ready to serve without detracting from the refined look of the living area.

With just enough room for the bare essentials, a simple bookshelf keeps the supplies for before-dinner cocktails close at hand and proves that a bar need not be a complicated affair. Having such a setup in the living area facilitates entertaining and cuts down on trips to the kitchen. ☊

Clustered around the fireplace, an inviting arrangement of sofa and chairs beckons guests to settle in and stay awhile. The French doors that line the left wall can be thrown open during the warmer months to allow guests the freedom of drifting between the yard and the indoor living space. ☋

keep in mind

- ☐ Patterned or textured upholstery will show spills less readily—an important consideration if you entertain frequently.

- ☐ Soft lighting is more flattering and creates an intimate ambience. Dimmers can be used to set the desired mood.

There's nothing like a hearth to enhance time spent with guests. This fireplace doubles as a room divider, creating an air of separation between the living area and the dining space while allowing the two to remain open to one another. The lowered ceiling over the dining area creates a cozier feeling there. ☊

The large deck that extends beyond the doors and windows of this living area increases the amount of gathering space for get-togethers during fair weather. No matter what the season, the soaring wall of glass visually expands the interior while providing a backdrop that is both soothing and spectacular. ↻

Set two steps down from the surrounding spaces and at the foot of a rustic hearth, this living room beckons visitors to prop up their feet and make themselves at home. When a crowd gathers, the set of nesting tables can be separated and distributed around the room, ensuring that all guests have a convenient surface on which to rest food and drinks. ☊

Just a few feet away, the kitchen is separated from the living area by a couple of steps and a work island. The floor plan allows hosts to remain in contact with their guests at all times—even when attending to last-minute preparations. An arched panel on the island keeps any clutter on the counter out of view from the living room. ♁

A skylight tucked into the vaulted ceiling invites sunshine into the kitchen.

Space Planning

We retreat to the living area for relaxation and various leisure-time **pursuits**. It is here that we engage in lively group discussions, sit down with a loved one for a heart-to-heart, gather together to play a board game, or snuggle up in a comfy chair to read a book. Fitting all these activities into a single room demands careful **planning**. Breaking the space down into multiple conversation areas and carving out **distinct** spots for specific pastimes will make time spent in the living area more enjoyable.

This room feels larger than its rather modest square footage would suggest because it includes two activity zones. The table and chairs at the far end of the room form a cozy setting for engaging in a tête-à-tête, savoring an afternoon snack, or doing a jigsaw puzzle. The main sitting area is perfect for enjoying a roaring fire on a winter day or simply catching up with family and friends. ➲

Clustered around a large coffee table, a pair of plush sofas and an inviting chair form the main sitting area of this living room. To the right, a second seating arrangement is grouped around an upholstered footrest. The latter configuration—smaller, somewhat secluded, and placed in front of a sunny bank of windows—sets an intimate mood, conducive to quiet conversation. ☊

In this living room, cushy love seats and chairs are strategically configured to encourage and facilitate conversation. The positioning of the seating also takes advantage of the fireplace as a focal point. A few steps away, a separate arrangement consisting of a table and chairs provides a spot for craft projects or games. The space demonstrates that well-planned furniture groupings can break up a large living room into defined activity areas. ◐

Divided visually by support beams, this vast room functions like two smaller ones. The sitting area in the foreground serves as an enticing spot in which to kick back and relax, while the billiards table beyond sets the stage for a game room. A smaller table to the left can hold refreshments or host a poker tournament. ♃

A large gathering area is enhanced by a snug alcove boasting a fireplace. Framed by a wide entrance and set off by a change in floor level, the round nook treats occupants of the living room to a pretty vignette. ☺

The charming alcove offers built-in seating, allowing occupants to bask in the warmth of the fire. Additional built-in features include shelves and cubbies, which provide space-efficient storage for books and wood. The setting is perfect for a romantic evening, quiet time with a book, or solitary contemplation. ➲

By making use of the space under the stairs, the owners were able to include a television and a stereo in the compact room.

Positioned in front of a fireplace, a trio of armchairs serves as an enticing gathering area. Eschewing the traditional couch, the arrangement has an appealingly fresh and relaxed look. Within the same space, an additional conversation area is formed by built-in seating arranged in an L-shape. Streamlined beneath massive windows and topped with cushions and toss pillows, the banquette also offers the opportunity to stretch out in the sun. ➲

Adjustable wall-mounted lamps are perfect above a banquette or sofa because they can easily be redirected as needed.

Geared for Children

Young children present a **unique** set of challenges for the living area. Brightly colored plastic toys often litter the floor (compromising a carefully composed design scheme in the process), spilled juice can stain rugs and upholstery, dainty furnishings are at risk of being damaged, and sharp corners pose safety hazards. By carefully planning your space—such as selecting furniture with rounded edges—you can avoid these undesirable occurrences. As a result, instead of succumbing to the potential chaos, your family room will be a comfortable **refuge** for children and adults alike.

bright ideas

▶ Protect upholstery with easy-wash slipcovers

▶ Display your children's works of art

▶ Choose a resilient, durable, easy-clean flooring material, such as a laminate

An alcove outfitted with built-in seating, a table, and two chairs gives grown-ups their own retreat while allowing them to keep an eye on the children.

The shallow drawer in this coffee table provides a convenient spot for keeping a few toys and books close at hand but neatly out of sight. Low enough to be reached safely by any youngster, the drawer can hold a rotating assortment of playthings. ↻

Surrounded by four child-size chairs, a typical coffee table becomes a perfect hub for the pint-size set. Sturdy and easy to clean, the table can stand up to the challenges dished out by children and can even provide a surface for arts-and-crafts projects. ↑

plan ahead

☐ Choose a matte finish for wood furnishings; this type of surface won't show fingerprints as readily

☐ Keep video and stereo equipment out of the reach of young, curious hands

Complete with built-in benches and plush, cushioned surfaces, this clever platform gives children a comfortable place to call their own. Drawers underneath the base of the unit keep belongings tidy and easily accessible. With a setup like this, the kids might even enjoy putting their toys away! ➲

A covered floor cushion and a generous supply of throw pillows are tucked into the recess underneath a staircase, creating a snug hideaway for reading, drawing, and quiet time. Treated to such a special spot, a child might even succumb to an impromptu nap. ☺

Good lighting—both natural and artificial—will ensure that any space, even the tiniest, looks warm and welcoming.

Entertainment Systems

Since its inception in the 1950s, the television has assumed an ever-increasing role in our lives. And as its importance has grown, so has its size. What's more, this ubiquitous amenity has gained a whole **entourage**, which can include a VCR, a DVD player, and speakers. And don't forget the stereo and its various components. In short, a hulking behemoth—the entertainment system—has invaded our homes. So how do you incorporate these **modern conveniences** into your living space without letting them take over the decor? **Creative** measures are required.

bright ideas

▶ Consider a built-in unit to streamline entertainment equipment

▶ Transform an attic into a media room

A shallow drawer keeps remote controls out of the way but readily accessible.

The stately design of this armoire conceals its state-of-the-art function: to store the components of a modern entertainment system, including television, VCR, and stereo. The most functional units include a shelf that pulls out and swivels so that the television can be adjusted for viewing from various angles. ◑

Thanks to its period styling, this built-in entertainment cabinet blends in seamlessly with the home's early American architecture. The setup just goes to show that a traditional home can play host to modern technology without compromising its aesthetic. ◑

Inspired by the styling of a centuries-old horse barn, the wooden cabinet doors built into the wall of this living room bring a touch of whimsy to the otherwise restrained decor. Thanks to the artful execution, many visitors might never guess the true purpose of this creative design feature. ◐

When the doors are opened, a complete entertainment system is revealed. Videos and CDs can be stored in the drawer underneath the television, allowing them to remain out of sight. Custom touches such as the star-shaped knobs on the drawer elevate the role of the cabinet beyond the purely practical. ◐

Notice how the doors slide back into the cabinet so that they don't obstruct anyone's view of the television.

Two media cabinets flanking the fireplace are built into a partial wall that serves as the divider between the living room and the adjacent space. Made from sealed maple, the finely crafted doors feature the same clean and simple lines that characterize the rest of the house. ↻

keep in mind

☐ For optimal sound, speakers should be raised off the ground. To keep them out of sight, recess them into a wall or the ceiling or include a place for them in the media cabinet

☐ The best viewing distance for a television is between two and two and a half times the width of the screen. If, for example, your television screen measures 28 inches (71cm) wide, the sofa should be located 56 to 70 inches (1.5–2m) back from it

The upper cabinet on the left opens to reveal the television and a speaker. An open grid at the top of the door allows fresh air to flow into the interior of the cabinet, preventing the buildup of heat that can be harmful to electronics. ☊

These sliding screens—adorned with eye-catching lattices of dark wood—move back and forth with the flick of a wrist. When the mammoth-size television is not in use, the panels can be moved into place to mask it. ↻

To prevent glare on the television screen, be sure to outfit all windows and glass doors with proper coverings.

When storage space is at a premium, a small chest can keep videocassettes out of the way while doubling as a side table.

Not every television must be hidden behind closed doors. This one, set atop a stylish cart, is small enough to maintain a low profile. Because the television rests on a rotating tray, viewers can adjust its position for a better view. ☊

Far more than a means to contain an entertainment system, this wall unit includes open compartments for displaying decorative objects.

Set into a wall-length stretch of built-in cabinetry, this enormous television screen looks far less assuming than it would otherwise. To maintain the neat appearance of the space, the cabinets include ample storage for the accessories that accompany media equipment, such as DVDs, CDs, and videocassettes. ☊

Positioned in a corner of this family room, the television can
be viewed comfortably from numerous spots. Taking advantage
of a corner in this fashion is also a space-efficient measure. ☊

Perfect for a serious film buff who wants to bring the movie-going experience home, this entertainment system features a large viewing screen and a separate projector—both suspended from the ceiling. The lighting in the room has been carefully arranged to eliminate glare. ☊

When the entertainment system is not in use, both the screen and the projector retract into the ceiling. One of the system's five speakers can be seen on the mantel that is sometimes concealed behind the screen. The others are placed to the sides and rear of the seating area, creating a surround-sound effect. ☊

Home Offices

A home office means different things to different people. Variations range from a small planning center used for organizing household paperwork to a full-fledged **workstation** designed to support a professional business endeavor. But function is not the only consideration that comes into play when a home office shares real estate with a living area. Such a work setup must not only accommodate the needs of its owners, but also **coordinate** with the decor of the surroundings. And there should be plenty of storage, so that papers and supplies don't clutter the overall appearance of the room.

This streamlined bank of cabinets offers more than just storage. Swing open the sets of doors above each of the chairs, and you'll discover two space-saving desks. Each one includes a work surface as well as access to a bank of drawers for storing files and supplies. ➲

Shelves accented with family photographs and decorative objects keep the wall unit in line with the living room decor.

While the hefty proportions, iron hardware, and careful detailing of this armoire lend it the look of a centuries-old antique, its interior is equipped with all the fittings of a twenty-first-century office. The desk that folds down offers plenty of room for a computer and keyboard, while storage space within the piece can accommodate a printer. Thanks to the strategic positioning of the armoire, owners can take advantage of a sunny view while working at home. ☊

A combination of cabinets and open shelving gives this desk an interesting facade. A unit such as this can hide a computer and still offer plenty of room for files and supplies. Here, numerous fabric-covered boxes provide pretty storage for office necessities while keeping the shelves tidy and organized. ↻

Thanks to its shallow depth, this secretary gives residents a place to do paperwork without taking up much space. The cabinet doors and fold-up desk grant owners the opportunity to hide all supplies and documents from view when they simply want to relax in the sitting area. A wicker chest doubling as a coffee table stands ready to hold any overflow of household files. ◑

The small writing surface offers a convenient spot for paying bills and keeping up with correspondence. Two modest-size drawers can hold pens and other supplies, while shelves up above provide a convenient home for books. Cabinets underneath the desk surface can hide bulkier items, such as ledgers and phone directories. ◓

Fireplaces and Hearths

ften the focal point of the living area, a fireplace merits careful design consideration. Wood burning or gas, contemporary or traditional, simple or dramatic, the choices abound. Furnishings should be arranged so that family members can comfortably soak in the warmth of a roaring fire and gaze upon the mesmerizing flames. Even when there isn't a blaze, the fireplace can retain its position as the center of attention with an eye-catching surround or intriguing decorative objects lined up along the mantel.

bright ideas

▶ Select an unusual mantelpiece, such as a piece of driftwood for a seaside home

▶ Change your mantel display with the seasons

The honey-colored woodwork that surrounds this fireplace provides as much visual warmth as the blaze itself. Built-in benches and bookshelves make fitting accompaniments, beckoning homeowners to abandon their chores and take it easy. ☊

The area above the mantel is a favorite place for showcasing artwork.

Tile flooring provides a low-maintenance surface for the hearth. While the floor tiles echo the bricks lining the inside of the fireplace, handmade tiles in a deep, cool, mottled green create a surround that is soothing to the eye. ♌

Located in the center of an otherwise open expanse, this fireplace helps to give the living area a feeling of intimacy. The deep ledge at the base provides additional seating. ⌒

Bordered on one side by a fireplace and on another by a floor-to-ceiling wall of bookshelves, this living space assumes a quiet, reflective mood. A large pillow provides cushioning for anyone who just wants to stretch out by the fire. ➲

Multifunctional, the fireplace not only fills the modest-size sitting area with warmth, but also visually separates it from the dining room. The result is a gathering space that feels snug but not claustrophobic. ➲

A low platform extends from the fireplace surround, providing an intriguing architectural detail and a place for displaying flowers or a basket of firewood.

A sunken living area creates a cozy setting in which to enjoy a fire. Practical as well as enticing, this design includes built-in benches and a storage compartment for several days' worth of wood. Topped with cushions and toss pillows, the benches offer comfortable perches. ↻

The mantelpiece that crowns this fireplace blends seamlessly with the cabinetry on either side of it. Simple and traditional, the handsome casework creates a stately look without seeming too imposing. An attractive iron rack stores an evening's supply of firewood close to the point of use. ➲

This contemporary inglenook offers an intimate spot in which to enjoy a fire. The openness of the design allows people in the larger gathering area to reap the benefits of the fireplace as well. ◑

Certain details encourage owners and guests to make use of the inglenook. Built-in shelves store books within arm's reach, while wall-mounted fixtures offer light for reading. ☉

Furnishings

Many homeowners enjoy the task of selecting and **arranging** furnishings more than any other step in the design process. After all, these are the elements that ultimately turn a house into a home and best represent the **personalities** of residents. Wherever your tastes lead you—traditional or contemporary, cozy or minimalist, thrift-store finds or department store splurges—remember to select your furnishings with an eye to your **lifestyle**. Pieces that suit how you spend your days are sure to please for years to come.

A variety of seating options gives residents and guests many choices in this living room. Two ottomans in front of the hearth allow occupants to enjoy the fire or to turn around and join in conversation with those seated on the sofas. In the foreground, two cushy chairs and a coffee table set slightly apart from the rest of the gathering space create a spot for a chat à deux while still allowing occupants to take part in group discussions. ➲

Casters on the armchairs and matching ottoman offer freedom of movement, allowing owners to easily change the positioning of these pieces as needed.

The garage-style door on this cabinet rolls up to reveal a convenient storage niche—perfect for a stereo.

Because built-in furniture features a lower profile than most freestanding pieces do, it is a good choice for small rooms. Here, a wrap-around sofa provides plenty of seating—without consuming very much space visually. The round pieces in front of it can be used either as side tables or for additional seating. ➲

Here, a built-in window seat takes advantage of a space that would otherwise go unnoticed. Though small in size, the nook plays a large role, lending a sense of quality craftsmanship to the room and providing an inviting spot for spending some time alone with a book—or simply with one's thoughts. ◯

Recessed directly into the wall, this built-in hutch provides ample storage and an attractive focal point without looking bulky or taking up too much space. Under-cabinet lighting illuminates treasures on display. ↻

When selecting furnishings, be sure to keep an open mind. In this room, a bench pulled up to the dining table provides extra seating in the living area when necessary. In addition, the bench allows the dining table to remain open to the rest of the modest-size space; chairs would have almost certainly closed it off. ∩

Accessorized with a large footrest and a floor lamp of just the right height, a leather chair in the corner of this living space beckons family members to settle down with a good book. A large upholstered ottoman can play many roles: as a footrest, as a surface for holding a tray of snacks, or as additional seating during get-togethers. ☯

Because this ottoman is placed on casters, it can be moved around the room easily, despite its hefty dimensions. The homeowners, for instance, could pull it over to the sofa to serve as a game table or roll it in front of the chair to prop up weary feet. ☯

Lighting

An often-overlooked element of room design, the lighting scheme is a subtle yet crucial feature that can reap a number of rewards. Not only can it create a mood, but it can also make a space function better. The key is to plan for a variety of light sources, some to brighten the entire space—known as ambient lighting—and others to provide direct illumination for specific activity-oriented areas—referred to as task lighting. Accent lighting can enhance the setting by illuminating artwork and other decorative objects, while such features as dimmers offer flexibility, allowing you to set the stage for a large, festive gathering or a quiet, romantic rendezvous.

Different types of fixtures work together to keep this open-plan room feeling light and airy. Sconces mounted high on the wall throw light onto the ceiling, creating an overall brightness that warms the room. Meanwhile, a floor lamp stationed by a comfortable chair provides illumination for reading. In the kitchen hidden behind the partial wall, pendant fixtures provide direct light for meal preparation. ➲

During the daytime, sunshine pours in through huge windows to provide most of the illumination in this room. Recessed fixtures discreetly shed light the rest of the time—without compromising the clean lines of the soaring wood-paneled ceiling. Finally, two sconces (one not shown in picture) cast light upwards, creating gentle layers of brightness. ∩

Small table lamps set into the recesses flanking this fireplace create an appealing soft glow while illuminating the diminutive decorative objects on display. If the lamps were not there, the tiny treasures would simply get lost in the two dark niches. Sconces on the wall above draw attention to the artwork displayed on the mantel. ☚

Perched atop a series of striking columns, these playful light fixtures are as eye-catching as they are illuminating. Thanks to their elevated position, they help to brighten the soaring ceiling, preventing it from looking like a black, gaping expanse during nighttime hours. ☛

To showcase the two treasured pieces of hanging artwork in this living room, mini-spotlights are suspended in front of them from the ceiling and concealed behind panels. Above the painting on the left, recessed lights shed even more illumination. Ambient light is provided by the two wall sconces. ☊

With a chair pulled into place, this sofa table is converted into a simple writing desk for paying bills or catching up on correspondence. A table lamp provides illumination for the task at hand.

Calling attention to the artwork they flank, these whimsical wall sconces provide gentle illumination. Without these fixtures, the charming sitting area—which has been carved out of the space underneath the stairs—would look dark and unwelcoming. A candle on a tall, spindly stand provides a natural complement. ♁

In the corner of this room, acrobatic figures suspended between two wires throw bits of light in every direction. Both the figures themselves and the light they cast are more artful than practical. Recessed fixtures in the ceiling shed a warm glow against the wall of red cabinetry. ☻

plan ahead

- ☐ Incorporate "layers" of light. Some fixtures should brighten the room overall, others should provide illumination for specific activities such as reading, and still others should spotlight treasured items like artwork or family photographs

- ☐ Install wall sconces above a reading chair. They take up less space—both physically and visually—than a floor lamp or a table lamp

Incorporating Color

Looking for a simple technique to breathe **new life** into your living area? Consider changing the color scheme. Paint the walls a soft yellow for a cheery effect, or reupholster your sofa in sage green for something more soothing. You can transform the look of a room with much smaller measures, too. Replace those cream-colored throw pillows with a few red ones, for instance, and you've created a **splash** of drama. Unsure which colors will work best? Trust your instincts, and select those that bring you the most pleasure.

bright ideas

- Have paint custom-blended to match a favorite piece of artwork
- Use different textures to enliven a monochromatic palette
- Paint the ceiling and trim the same color as the walls to visually enlarge the room

Almost the color of butternut squash at the peak of ripeness, the orange-yellow walls of this living area wrap occupants in autumnal coziness. To provide refreshing contrast, the crown moldings and window trim are set off in crisp white paint. ⟁

The color scheme of a room can be used to set a mood. Here, a pale green backdrop and a weathered trunk stained a restful shade of blue create a peaceful ambience. Cool hues such as these are prized for their calming effect. ⋂

Decked out in red and yellow,
shutterlike accents flanking
the pass-through add pizzazz.
Thanks to the open floor plan,
the colorful accessories can be
appreciated from the living area.

Color is also an effective tool for defining different activity
zones. In this open floor plan, a wall of robin's egg blue lends
an air of distinction to the transition area between the foyer and
the living space. For a sense of continuity, a sliver of the same
hue extends into the sitting area, which is full of neutrals. ☮

This room's primarily cream-colored decor allows the vivid hues of the painting to shine in all their glory. As a result, the piece of art takes center stage. Decorative accents—from the toss pillows to the vases—take their cues from the painting. ☉

Even the window shades are white so as not to detract from the art.

A ceiling fan needn't be purely functional. This one adds an extra dash of color to the space.

In this living area, sunny yellow paint draws the eye toward the fireplace, allowing the traditional focal point to hold its own against the breathtaking views provided by vast expanses of windows. The warm hue injects a powerful sense of energy into the space. ☾

Don't forget about surfaces overhead when it comes to color. Painted red, the canopy establishes a sense of intimacy.

In a living room filled with white walls, a crimson panel draws attention to the entertainment system. Reminiscent of a theater's red curtains, the panel creates a dramatic backdrop for the drama on the screen. ➲

Soft Touches

In today's fast-paced, high-tech world, the living area serves as a nurturing refuge—an oasis of comfort. While the layout, architectural features, and furnishings all set the stage for your activities, it's the softer touches—the upholstery, the window treatments, and the floor coverings—that provide tactile and visual pleasure, not to mention a sense of finish. Of course, these design details have practical attributes as well. Window treatments provide shade and privacy, and rugs supply warmth and cushioning underfoot.

bright ideas

▶ Rotate slipcovers with the seasons

▶ Let curtains cascade to the floor to make the ceiling look higher

▶ Use one pattern throughout a small room to make it seem larger

With its soft texture, a chenille throw speaks of comfort and pampering. The much-appreciated accessory not only promises to wrap occupants in warmth and coziness, but also gives the sofa a dash of color. Even the color—a deep olive green—looks rich and inviting. ➲

A flowering plant enlivens a formerly stark corner.

Slipcovers offer a number of benefits. They can be thrown in the wash or sent to the dry cleaner when soiled, and they can be changed to give a room a new look. Here, the fabrics chosen for the slipcovers pick up the hues of the rag rug and offer smooth contrast to the floor covering's nubby texture. ♌

In a room resplendent with color, bamboo shades provide a neutral but nonetheless warm accent. The texture and coloring of the window treatments work well with the space's wood detailing. ♌

A miniature wagon becomes a novel storage device for magazines.

To add interest to a large expanse of wall, choose a subtly textured wall covering instead of plain paint.

Covering only the lower portion of the windows, semisheer shades create some privacy for the occupants of this living area while still allowing them to enjoy the view. The trim, minimalist demeanor of the window treatments matches the clean lines of the loft while offering a softening counterpoint to the space's industrial design. ☊

While minimalist venetian blinds shade this living room from harsh sunlight, a colorful valance injects a jaunty note worthy of the surroundings. Notice how this festive window treatment incorporates the color scheme and sharply defined angles present in the rest of the space. ⌒

Bringing nature inside will help create a peaceful setting.

keep in mind

☐ Upholstery should feel as good as it looks, so be sure to touch samples before settling on final selections

☐ Remember that you will often view your room from a distance. When selecting fabrics for furniture, accessories, and window treatments, observe patterns from several feet away as well as up close

A natural-fiber rug makes a fitting companion for a trio of wicker chairs in this pleasant sitting area. The numerous earthy textures give the space a soothing quality. ☻

Displaying Treasures

ollecting is a favorite pastime for many of us. And part of the pleasure comes from putting our **cherished** objects on display. But the means of display requires careful consideration. If not treated properly, a collection can look cluttered and fussy or simply get lost in the mix. Placement, arrangement, and backdrop all affect the **impact** that your treasures will have. When displayed conscientiously, a group of vintage teapots or black-and-white photographs can turn into an eye-catching design element and a sure conversation starter.

bright ideas

▶ Browse through your belongings for the makings of a new collection

▶ Mount an assortment of decorative plates on the wall instead of traditional artwork

▶ Employ freestanding open shelving to double as an airy room divider

In a compact room, a simple shelf affixed to the wall can provide a place to showcase photographs and art without eating up valuable space. In this artful display, a tall vase on the right counterbalances the tall frame and lamp on the left. ☊

Picture rails keep this photography collection looking orderly. Since the framed photographs are not affixed to the wall, they can be rotated easily and frequently for an ever-changing scene. ↻

Spice up a grouping of photographs by having a few mounted on mats of a different color. Black-and-white or sepia-toned images in particular will stand out against a colored background.

The shelves flanking this fireplace are as much works of art as the items they showcase. Soft shades of green, red, and yellow distinguish the different compartments from one another and provide flattering backdrops for the objects on display. Meanwhile, gently curving lines lend the pieces a modern sophistication. ↻

Composed of bulbous shapes in various sizes and materials, this vignette demonstrates a decorating truth: when similar items are grouped together, they assume an artistic quality and pack a definite design punch. If the same items were scattered about the room, they might go unnoticed. ☙

A bright yellow backdrop energizes this whimsical collection of vintage vases. Contributing a variety of heights and hefts, the vases are clustered together to give the impression of a single design element. While the individual pieces come in different materials, textures, and scales, they share simple, clean lines, making them good display partners. ➲

A low coffee table will consume less visual space than a taller one, preserving the sense of openness in a room.

A creative designer retrofitted the interior of this antique armoire to showcase a collection of miniature furnishings. To protect the precious contents from dust and the damaging rays of the sun, the owner can simply shut the doors. ↻

Because the pieces are displayed within their own compartments, they stand out more as individuals and garner more attention than they would if simply clustered together on a shelf. For a charmingly coordinated look, the country style of the armoire mimics that of the collectibles. ☻

Storage

Most of us are waging a constant battle against the ever-growing tide of **paraphernalia** that enters our homes. From books and magazines to CDs and videocassettes to toys and craft supplies, the onslaught never seems to cease. Without a place of their own, these innocuous items can wreak havoc in a living area, making it look cluttered and unwelcoming. Thankfully, today there are plenty of clever storage **options** that can be tailored to your particular needs.

bright ideas

▶ Consider built-in storage for space efficiency

▶ Incorporate decorative storage options, such as vintage suitcases

A built-in storage unit makes efficient use of the wall space beneath a second-story loft. The accommodating configuration includes room for the entertainment system and decorative objects, as well as hidden storage for unsightly items. A coat closet off to the side completes the practical design. ➲

The bookshelves running along one end of this living area double as a room divider, creating a partition between the sunken sitting area and the adjacent hallway. Cabinets at the bottom mask unattractive items, while open shelves prominently display books, family photographs, and collectibles. In addition, custom-designed compartments hold the television, speakers, and wood for the fireplace. ↻

A simple bench situated beneath a window turns a passageway into a pleasant alternative sitting area.

This window seat performs double duty, providing both a place to stretch out and convenient storage space. Because the cubbies are accessible from the front of the bench instead of the top, the contents can be retrieved without removing the pillows and cushion that cover the seat. ↻

A white border lends a sense of finish and definition to wall-to-wall carpeting.

A nonworking fireplace can play host to decorative storage devices, like these two large wicker baskets. Taking advantage of what would otherwise be wasted space, the baskets not only help keep the room tidy, but also prevent the hearth from seeming like a dark void. ➲

Similar in shape but not exact duplicates, the earth-toned baskets are as eye-catching as they are practical. Thanks to their lids, the contents remain hidden from view, thereby creating a neater appearance than that of open baskets. The tops also provide surfaces for stacking books or displaying decorative objects. ➲

An antique chest used as a coffee table not only adds charm to this living area, but also offers storage space for such bulky items as photo albums, blankets, and board games. Incorporating furnishings that perform more than one function will help to save space and cut down on clutter. ○

The drawers built into this coffee table provide storage for items right at their point of use. Thanks to these handy features, everything from remote controls and coasters to decks of cards and other games can be stashed within arm's reach. The shallow design of the drawers allows the contents to be retrieved easily. ☝

Outdoor Elements

 glimpse of greenery, an expanse of blue sky, a few unharnessed beams of sunlight. Scientists have recently documented a fact that we have all long known to be true: Mother Nature has the power to **lift the spirits** and calm the soul. Because of these effects, the most pleasing living areas are the ones that **embrace the outdoors.** In such rooms, a wall of French doors might open onto a deck, or a picture window might show off a breathtaking view. Limited by space? Even a single skylight can blur the line between indoors and out.

Airy fanlights top a pair of French doors to let in additional natural light and contribute a decorative flair. Notice how the shape of these crowning details echoes the arch of the nearby casement window. ➲

An interior window allows light to flow from the living room into a second-story bedroom. If the sunshine gets to be too much or if privacy is desired, the shutters can simply be closed.

Casement windows and accompanying transoms flood this room with natural light, but it's the enormous round window up above that steals the show. Tucked into the peak of a soaring ceiling, this architectural attention-grabber not only provides a striking focal point, but also ensures that the upper portion of the two-story room remains light during daytime hours. ⋂

keep in mind

☐ Well-insulated windows not only regulate indoor air temperature, but also muffle outside sounds

☐ Skylights that detect inclement weather and automatically close when necessary are now available

With large expanses of glass covering much of the walls and part of the ceiling, this open-plan space treats its occupants to an abundance of sunlight and large swatches of blue sky. An architectural design such as this invites nature to become a part of everyday life. ☚

A wall of windows wraps around a corner of this living area, providing a view of the adjacent patio. Sliding glass doors permit easy movement between the indoor and outdoor gathering spaces, allowing the two to merge. A glass panel bridging the gap between the top of the patio doors and the ceiling virtually disappears, creating the illusion that the space is open. ☻

The way in which the roofline continues from indoors to outdoors further causes the two spaces to appear as one.

At the other end of the room, the theme of floor-to-ceiling glass continues. Treated to a phenomenal view, dinner guests can enjoy the feeling (if not the reality) of an alfresco meal—no matter what Mother Nature decides to dish out. On a comfortably warm evening, glass-paned doors invite guests to spill outside for cocktails or coffee. ➲

A sisal rug suits this setting, in which so much emphasis is placed on the natural landscape.

Shelves built into a stretch of floor-to-ceiling windows offer a novel approach to showing off prized collectibles. What's more, the display setup enhances the glass objects, allowing sunlight to make their colors and forms come alive. ➲

Virtually free of embellishment, the floor-to-ceiling walls of glass that wrap around this living area are almost invisible to the eye. As a result, the interior space seems to become one with the natural surroundings. ◑

A dropped lighting panel over the living area creates a sense of intimacy.

Two Asian-style screens lend visual interest to one of the walls of glass. Stylish and practical, these translucent panels provide some relief from the bright sun without blocking the light altogether. ↻

Resources

Information and Products

If you are interested in hiring a qualified professional to help with a remodeling job or new construction, here is a list of design and planning resources that may be helpful:

American Institute of Architects (AIA)—When making structural changes, an architect should be considered. Many, but not all, architects belong to The American Institute of Architects. Call (202) 626-7300 for information and the phone number of your local chapter. www.aiaonline.com

The American Society of Interior Designers (ASID)—An interior designer can provide helpful advice, especially when remodeling an existing space. The American Society of Interior Designers represents over 20,000 professionally qualified interior designers. Call ASID's client/referral service at (800) 775-ASID. www.asid.org

National Association of the Remodeling Industry (NARI)—When it's time to select a contractor to work on your project, you might consider a member of the National Association of the Remodeling Industry. Call (800) 611-6274 for more information. www.nari.org

National Association of Home Builders (NAHB)—When you're looking at builders to construct a new home, contact the National Association of Home Builders. Call (800) 368-5242 for more information. www.nahb.org

The following manufacturers, associations, and resources may be helpful as you plan your living area:

GENERAL

Home Depot
(800) 430-3376
www.homedepot.com

Lowe's
(800) 44-LOWES
www.lowes.com

FABRIC & WALL COVERINGS

Brunschwig & Fils
www.brunschwig.com

Eisenhart Wall Coverings
(800) 726-3267

Imperial Wall Coverings
(800) 539-5399
www.imp-wall.com

Waverly
(800) 423-5881
www.waverly.com

FLOORING

www.floorfacts.com
(a global directory that helps consumers explore flooring options)

Italian Trade Commission
Ceramic Tile Department
499 Park Avenue
New York, NY 10022
(212) 980-1500
www.italtrade.com

National Wood Flooring
Association
16388 Westwoods Business
Park
Ellisville, MO 63021
(800) 422-4556
www.woodfloors.org

Pergo
(800) 33-PERGO
www.pergo.com

FURNISHINGS AND ACCESSORIES

Arhaus
(866) 427-4287
www.arhaus.com

Baker Furniture
(800) 59-BAKER
www.bakerfurniture.com

Broyhill Furniture Industries
(800) 3-BROYHILL

Century Furniture
(828) 328-1851
www.centuryfurniture.com

Crate & Barrel
(800) 967-6696
www.crateandbarrel.com

Ethan Allen
(800) 228-9229
www.ethanallen.com

Harden Furniture
(315) 245-1000
www.harden.com

Hold Everything
(800) 840-3596
www.holdeverything.com

Ikea
(800) 225-IKEA
www.ikea.com

Lexington Home Furnishings
(800) 539-4636
www.lexington.com

Mitchell Gold Company
(800) 789-5401
www.mitchellgold.com

Pier 1 Imports
(800) 447-4371
www.pier1.com

Pottery Barn
(800) 922-5507
www.potterybarn.com

Room & Board
(800) 486-6554
www.roomandboard.com

Rowe Furniture
(800) 334-7693
www.rowefurniture.com

Sauder Furniture
(800) 523-3987
www.sauder.com

Scott Jordan Furniture
(212) 620-4682
www.scottjordan.com

Spiegel
(800) SPIEGEL
www.spiegel.com

Thomasville
(800) 927-9202
www.thomasville.com

LIGHTING

American Lighting Association
(800) 274-4484
www.americanlightingassoc.com

Virtual Lighting Designer
from GE
www.gelighting.com

PAINT

Benjamin Moore
(800) 6-PAINT 6
www.benjaminmoore.com

Dutch Boy
(800) 828-5669
www.dutchboy.com

Pratt & Lambert
www.prattandlambert.com

Sherwin-Williams
(800) 474-3794
www.sherwin-williams.com

WINDOWS & DOORS

Andersen
(800) 426-4261
www.andersenwindows.com

Hunter Douglas Window
Fashions
(800) 937-7895
www.hunterdouglas.com

Loewen
(800) 245-2295
www.loewen.com

Marvin
(800) 241-9450
www.marvin.com

Morgan
(800) 877-9482
www.morgandoors.com

Pella
(800) 54-PELLA
www.pella.com

Pozzi
(800) 257-9663
www.pozzi.com

Photo Credits

Beateworks/www.beateworks.com:
©Tim Street-Porter: pp. 20-21, 26,
50-51, 55

©Philip Beaurline/
www.beaurline.com: pp. 96-97

©Bjorg/www.bjorgphoto.com: pp.
84 (Designer: Bonaventura), 88
top (Designer: Bonaventura)

Elizabeth Whiting Associates:
©Neil Lorimer, p. 70

©Tria Giovan: pp. 63, 65, 71 top,
71 bottom, 101, 105, 106, 107, 110,
111, 115 top, 115 bottom

©Nancy Hill: pp. 44 (Designer:
Gunklemans Interior Design,
MN), 117 (Designer: Deborah T.
Lipner Interior Design, CT)

©Timothy Hursley: pp. 120-121
(Architect: Frank O. Gehry)

Interior Archive: ©Tim Beddow,
pp. 48 (Designer: Giles & Bella
Gibbs), 49 (Designer: Giles &
Bella Gibbs); ©Wayne Vincent, p.
12 (Architect: Clinton Pritchard)

©David Duncan Livingston/
www.davidduncanlivingston.com:
pp. 2, 30, 31, 69, 85 top, 104, 124,
125

©Mark Lohman: pp. 17 (Architect:
Douglas Burdge; Stylist: Sunday
Hendrickson), 27 (Architect:
Douglas Burdge; Stylist: Sunday
Hendrickson), 36 (Designer:
Darren Henault), 60 (Architect:

Harry Topping; Stylist: Sunday
Hendrickson), 61 (Architect:
Harry Topping; Stylist: Sunday
Hendrickson), 62 (Designer: Ria
Jacobs; Stylist: Robin Tucker), 64
(Architect: William Hefner;
Stylist: Laura Hill), 95, 102
(Designer: Janet Lohman), 114
(Designer: Katheryne Designs;
Stylist: Sunday Hendrickson)

©Undine Prohl: p. 35 (Architect:
Natalye Appel)

Red Cover: ©Graham Atkins-
Hughes, pp. 34, 98-99, 109 bottom;
©Andreas von Einsiedel, pp.80, 109
top; ©Chris Evans, pp. 10, 32; ©Jake
Fitzjones, pp. 13; ©Ken Hyden, p.
103 (Designer: Jonathan Reed);
©Verity Welstead, p. 54

©Eric Roth/
www.ericrothphoto.com: pp. 11, 16
(Architect: John Chapman), 38
(Designer: Gayle Mandle), 39
(Designer: Gayle Mandle), 46,
82(Architect & Designer: Peter
Wheeler), 85 bottom (Architect:
Heather Wells), 92 (Designer &
Stylist: Gregor D. Cann)

©Mark Samu/
www.samustudios.com: pp. 8
(Courtesy Hearst Publications,
Stylist: Margaret McNicholas) 33
(Courtesy Hearst Publications,
Stylist: Tia Burns), 56 (Courtesy
Hearst Publications, Stylist:
Margaret McNicholas), 74
(Courtesy Hearst Publications,

Architect: Peter Cook; Stylist:
Margaret McNicholas), 87
(Architect: Sears & Sears;
Designer: Jeanne Leonard
Interiors), 89 (Designer: Beverly
Balk), 93, 100 (Courtesy Hearst
Publications, Architect: Val Florio;
Stylist: Margaret McNicholas)

©Claudio Santini/
www.claudiosantini.com: pp. 86
(Architect: House & House), 88
bottom (Architect: Peter Wormser
+ Associates), 91 (Designer: Linda
Applewhite & Associates)

©Brad Simmons/
www.bradsimmons.com: pp. 47
(Builder: Oakbridge Timber
Framing; Stylist: Joetta Moulden;
Owner: Richard & Judy
Thompson), 58 (Owner: Courtney
& Greg Blackman), 59 (Owner:
Courtney & Greg Blackman), 112
(Architect: Scott L. Barton;
Builder: Steve Shauger, Peter
Blackledge; Owner: Lindsay &
Lennie MacArthur)

©Tim Street-Porter: pp. 53
(Designer: Lisa Stanton), 94, 108
(Designer: Scott Johnson)

©Brian Vanden Brink: pp. 6, 14
(Architect: Mark Hutker
Associates), 15 (Architect: Mark
Hutker Associates), 22 (Architect:
Brett Dunham), 23 (Architect:
Brett Dunham), 28 (Architect:
Centerbrook Architects), 29

(Architect: Centerbrook
Architects), 37 (Designer: IO
Oakes), 40 (Architect: Allen
Freysinger; Designer: Christina
Oliver), 41 (Architect: Allen
Freysinger; Designer: Christina
Oliver), 42 (Architect: Lo Yi
Chan), 43 (Architect: Lo Yi Chan),
45 (Designer: Drysdale
Associates), 66 (Designer:
Custom Electronics), 67
(Designer: Custom Electronics),
68 (Architect: Pete Bethanis), 72
(Architect: Lynn Perry), 73
(Architect: Lynn Perry), 75 top
(Architect: Richard Burt), 75 bot-
tom (Architect: Richard Burt), 76
(Architect: Richard Burt), 77
(Architect: Mark Hutker
Associates), 78 (Architect: Winton
Scott), 79 (Architect: Winton
Scott), 83 (Builder: South
Mountain Builders), 90
(Designer: Drysdale Associates),
113 (Architect: Peter Rose), 116
(Architect: Stepher Blatt), 119
(Architect: Tom Catalano)

©Dominique Vorillon: pp. 18
(Architect: Glen Irani), 19
(Architect: Glen Irani), 25, 81
(Architect: Glen Irani), 118
(Designer: Roy McMakin), 122
(Architect/Owner: Mark Rios), 123
top (Architect/Owner: Mark Rios),
123 bottom (Architect/Owner:
Mark Rios)

©Jessie Walker: pp. 24, 52, 57

Index